Candle of the Vampire

DELUXE ADVENTURE MODULE

The Lord Vultaric Chronicles V.2

An Adventure Module for 1 Player
For the Hammer + Cross RPG
Designed by Noah Patterson

Hammer

Cross

Candle of the Vampire
The Lord VanDrac Chronicles V.2

Copyright © 2020 Noah Patterson
ISBN: 9798689673851

Find us on DriveThru RPG
Or at MicroRPG.weebly.com

Cover Artwork by Dean Spencer Art

Map Art by Patrick E. Pullen

STOP!

DON'T BUY THIS BOOK!
At least, not yet.

The basic rules for the Micro Chapbook RPG system and Hammer + Cross found in this book can be downloaded for FREE through DriveThruRPG.com in the Manor of Blood book. Give the system a try before you buy.

With that in mind, this Deluxe Adventure Module includes everything you need to play the game.

You don't need any other book to experience the game!

Contents

1.0: What is Candle of the Vampire?

2.0: What You Need

3.0: Basic Rules

4.0: Adventure Background

5.0: The Woods

6.0: Ivrad

    6.1: The Crow's Inn

7.0: The Holy Father Cathedral

    7.1: The Bell Tower

8.0: Ending the Adventure

Section 1.0

What is Candle of the Vampire?

Candle of the Vampire is an adventure module for the Hammer + Cross Roleplaying game system and is the second volume in the Lord VanDrac Chronicles story arc. Each volume in the 5 book series stands on its own, but all connect to create a greater campaign. Therefore, this adventure can be played on its own or as part of the larger VanDrac story arc.

This book includes the basic rules to allow you to play the game. However, the Hammer + Cross core rulebook will go into greater detail on all elements of the game. Hammer +

Cross uses the Micro Chapbook RPG system and, therefore, this book can be combined with any other books or genres in the same system.

For those new to the system, Micro Chapbook RPG is an ultra-rules light fantasy-based game designed specifically for the solitaire gamer in mind--but is adaptable for co-op play as well as traditional Game Master driven gameplay.

Hammer + Cross is a Gothic Horror rendition of the traditionally fantasy-based game system. In Hammer + Cross, you take on the role of vampire and monster hunters in an alternate version of late 1800s Victorian Europe where evil abounds. The game is strongly influenced by the Hammer Horror films of the 60s and 70s.

Section 2.0

What Do You Need?

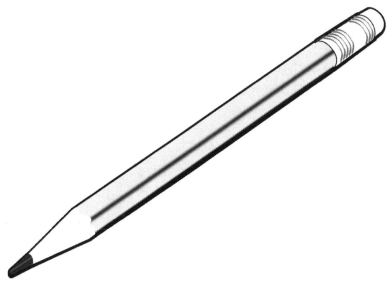

To play this adventure you will need:

- A Pencil and Eraser
- A Sheet of Graph Paper
- A Character Sheet
- 2 Six-Sided Dice
- This Adventure Book
- The Hammer + Cross Core Rulebook (Optional).

Section 3.0

Rules Basics

Hammer + Cross is an ultra-simple roleplaying game that can be played solo (or with a traditional GM if you so wish). In the next few pages, you will find the basic rules for the game system:

What You Need: 2 six-sided dice, graph paper, notepaper/character sheet, a pencil w/eraser, Scenario Maps/Sticker, this chapbook.

Rolling: During play, you always roll 1D6, trying to score equal to or lower than your stat score. If you are proficient, roll 2 dice and take the better result of the 2. 1 always succeeds. 6 always fails. (NOTE: When you see 1D3 it means you roll a die and half the result rounding up. 1D2 means: Odds = 1, Evens = 2.)

Characters: To create a character, do the following:

1. **STATS:** You have 4 statistics. **ST**rength, **DE**xterity, **WI**ts, **CH**arisma. You have 7 points to assign between them as you see fit (9 for an easier game). No stat can have a score lower than 1 or higher than 4 at this point.

2. **CLASS:** Choose a class. There are 4 to choose from. Each one will make you proficient in one area.
   a. **Soldier:** Proficient in ST
   b. **Hunter:** Proficient in DE
   c. **Nurse/Doctor:** Proficient in WI
   d. **Priest/Nun:** Proficient in CH

3. **ORDER:** Choose an Order to join. Your Order grants you a +1 bonus to one stat.
   a. **Order of the Hammer:** +1 ST
   b. **Order of the Dagger:** +1 DE
   c. **Order of the Cross:** +1 WI
   d. **Order of the Sun:** +1 CH
4. **HEALTH, WILL, & FAITH:** Your health is your ST+DE+20. Your will is your WI+CH+20. Your Faith is your Wits + 20 (+ 25 if you're a Priest/Nun).

Weapons: Roll 2D6 to determine your money. You may buy equipment now. Weapons have a damage rating and a cost in pounds (£). Below are some basic starter weapons, both ranged and melee. You may have 2 melee and 1 ranged at any given time. You may buy these and others in town as well.

Melee Weapons			Ranged Weapons		
Dagger	1	1g	Holy Cross	1	2g
Wooden Stake	1D3	2g	Holy Water Sprayer	1D3	3g
Hammer	1D3+1	3g	Rusty Revolver	1D3+1	5g
Cane Sword	1D6	4g	Blessed Long Whip	1D6	6g
Silver Sword	1D6+1	5g	Crossbow	1D6+1	7g

Armor and Items: Armor grants the wearer a boost to their health, will, or both. Other items such and food and potions can be used to restore lost health and will. On the next page are some basic starter items and armors. You may buy these and others in town as well.

Armor			Items		
Shield	+3H	1£	(2) Bread Crust	1D3 H	1£
Top Hat	+3W	1£	(3) Wine	1D3 W	1£
Black Cloak	+6H	2£	(4) Steak Meal	1D6 H	2£
Chainmail	+6W	2£	(5) Holy Water	1D6 W	2£
Blessed Robes	+6HW	3£	(6) Miracle	FULL HW	6£

Generating Rooms: Begin by choosing a random square on the graph paper and generating the first room. To generate a room, roll 2D6. The number rolled in the number of squares in the room. These can be drawn in any way, shape, or form so long as they are orthogonally connected. Next, roll 1D3 (1D6 divided by 2 rounded up). This is the number of NEW doors in the room (not including the door you just came through). Draw small rectangles to represent the doors along any single square's edge to designate an exit.

Room Type: Each newly generated room has a type. Roll 1D6 on the scenario Room Chart to determine the type. Note this in the room with the type's letter code as listed on the chart.

Doorways: Next, you will choose one door to move through into the next room. Roll 1D6 to determine the door type. After moving, generate the new room. (This chart is also provided in each scenario).

(5-6)	Unlocked	Move through freely.
(4)	Stuck	Must make a ST check to get through. Lose 1 WILL to reroll and try again.
(3)	Locked	Must make a WI check to get through. Lose 1 WILL to reroll and try again.
(1-2)	Trapped	Must make a WI check to disarm and move. If you fail, take 1D3 damage but still move through.

Monsters: After Entering any room. Roll to generate the monsters in the room. Roll once for the monster type (on the scenario Monster Chart) and a second time for the number of that monster. Each monster has a Max number of that type that can appear in a room, a Health Damage, a Will Damage, and a Life Force. **Vampires** also have two additional special stats:

- **Bloodletting (BL):** Each time the player rolls a 6 during a melee attack (an instant failure), the vampire bites them and drinks their blood. The BL is how much LF it regains.
- **Power (P):** This is the mental strength of the vampire. It is the amount of faith the player will lose if they fail during the Faith check.

Fighting: To fight the monsters in your room, follow these steps in order:

1. **Bravery:** Make a CH check. If you pass, gain 1 Will. If you fail, you lose Will according to the monster's W DMG. If your Will is ever 0, all rolls take a +1 modifier. (A roll of 1 STILL always succeeds)
2. **Ranged Attack:** IF the room is 4 squares or larger you may make a ranged attack. Roll a DE check. If you succeed, apply weapon damage to the monster's LF.

3. **Melee Attack:** You MUST now make a melee attack using a ST check. If you succeed, apply the weapon's damage to the monster's LF. If you fail, roll the H DMG for one monster and apply it to your health. If you have a second melee weapon equipped, attack again.
4. **Repeat:** Repeat this entire process until either you die or you've killed all the monsters in the room. Run away with a successful CH roll.

Faith Check: After battle, if the player was bitten by a vampire during combat, that player makes a WI check. If the player fails, they lose Faith in the amount of the vampire's power. The player may spend 1 Willpower to reroll this check. If Faith reaches 0, the character dies and becomes a vampire.

Search: After battle roll 1D6. If you get 1 through 5 you earn that much money. If you roll a six, roll on the Items table included in the scenario (or the one here in this section. The number to the left of each item is the search roll number). If you roll a 1 on the items chart you find nothing.

The Boss: The boss of the dungeon will not appear until you've encountered all the other monsters in the scenario at least once. Additionally, it will only appear in specific room types as outlined in each scenario. If you roll the boss when it can't appear, reroll. Once the boss is defeated, the game ends.

Alternate Boss Rule: (for potentially quicker games) Keep track of each monster you kill during the dungeon. After each battle is won, roll 2D6. If the roll is LOWER than the number of monsters killed during the dungeon, the boss can now have a chance of appearing. The boss will only appear in specific areas, as designated by the scenario rules. If you roll the boss when it can't appear, reroll.

Leveling Up: In between games you may spend 100 gold to add +1 to one stat (or 50 for an easier game). No stat can be higher than 5. For an easier game, simply level up whenever you defeat a boss. You may also buy new equipment. You may only have 2 melee and 1 ranged weapon at a time.

Section 4.0
Adventure Background

After solving the mystery at Mother's Light Convent, and killing the vampire there, you return to your Order's headquarters in London only to be immediately assigned to a new investigation out in the countryside. You argue with your superior that your work with Mother's Light isn't finished. After all, you were hoping for a little time to peruse the Order's library for any information on who Lord VanDrac is. Unfortunately, your superior insists that this new investigation is far more important. It seems there are some strange goings on at a small town cathedral to the north of the city.

Once again, you step out onto the cobblestone street to await your carriage. The chill of autumn hangs in the air and orange leaves from the park across the way blow toward your feet. Pulling your jacket around you, you see the carriage coming. Climbing in, you prepare for a day's long journey.

Dozing off, you wake as the carriage stops in a wooded area of the country. "Out," the driver says rudely without climbing down. Opening the door, you step out, your foot crunching down on a thick carpet of leaves along the dirt road.

"My bags?" you ask the driver. He responds by tossing them haphazardly from the top and, before you can protest his lack of professionalism, he has taken the reins and ridden off, speeding in a wide circle and taking off back toward London—a wave of leaves kicking up behind him. You stand there is awe, realizing this is the second time he has quickly dropped you off and ridden away as fast as possible.

Irritably picking up your bag from the dirt and brushing it off, you take your first real look around. You quickly realize there are no buildings in sight. It seems the driver has left you in the middle of nowhere.

Section 5.0

The Woods

Something definitely seems off about this investigation. First of all, this is the second time the driver has been quick to drop you and leave. Worse than that, he dropped you in the woods when you were supposed to be visiting an old cathedral. Taking out the notes your superior gave you on this case, you see he included a map. If you are correct in your estimations, it looks like you're not too far from the town and cathedral. It should be just a half hour walk through the woods. However, you better hurry. The sun is already setting.

Woods Special Rules:

<u>Setting Sun</u>: After completing each area, record 1 sunset point. The number of points pertains to how dark it is and how dangerous it is out in the woods. There is a modifier you will apply to your monster roll as well as a modifier to all your stat rolls.

SUNSET POINTS								
0	1	2	3	4	5	6	7	8
MONSTER ROLL MODIFIER								
0	0	+1	+1	+2	+2	+3	+3	+3
STAT ROLL MODIFIER								
0	0	0	+1	+1	+1	+1	+2	+2

<u>Navigation</u>: After completing each area, make a WITS check. If you pass, record one "Navigation" point. Then roll 2D6. If the result of the combined dice roll is lower than the number of Navigation points you've currently earned, you find your way out of the woods and into the small town of Ivrad.

<u>Doorways and Rooms</u>: The term doorways is replaced with "Exits" for the woods. Rooms is replaced with "Areas"

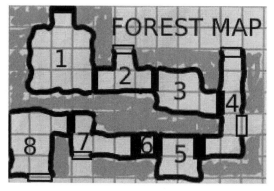

When mapping outdoor dungeons, there is an added element to creating "rooms" (or better known as areas in this instance). Each time you generate a new area, and after rolling the doors (called exits in this instance), the area directly around it must be shaded in to show the local foliage--all adjacent squares except the ones leading to exits are shaded. In the woods, you might use a green or grey colored pencil to show the trees.

In the example above, you can see how a player might roll through 8 areas of the map. Each has shading around it. However, you are free to build rooms directly adjacent to pre drawn shading--so long as there is at least 1 row of shading between areas where exits aren't connecting them.

Woods Exits

6	Clear	Move through freely.
5	Muck	Must make a ST check to tread through the mud. If you fail, lose 1 WILL and reroll and try again.
4	Blocked	A bramble of low branches or a fallen tree block the way. Make a DE check to leap over. If you fail, lose 1 HEALTH and reroll to try again.
3	Twisted Path	Must make a WI check to navigate the path. If you fail, lose 1 WILL and reroll and try again.
2	Tunnel	Brambles, rocks, and branches have fallen or grown here creating a dank and dark tunnel you must crawl through. Make a CH check to gain enough bravery to get on your hands and knees to crawl through. If you fail, you may spend 1 Willpower to try again.
1	Falling Branches	When you move through, an old tree branch falls down upon you. Make a DE check to dodge it or take 1D2 damage.

\multicolumn{3}{c}{**Woods Area Types**}		

1	**Clearing**	C	This area is clear, with a carpet of crunchy leaves on the ground, and light can shine through the canopy. No effect.
2	**Grave**	G	You stumble upon a grave, marked with a shoddy cross or crumbling gravestone. As you move through, moldy hands spring up from the dirt trying to grab your ankles. Before each round of combat make a DE check. If you fail, the hands trip you. All attacks for this turn are made at +2 and all monster damage is increased by 1.
3	**Pit**	P	A large pit sits in this area. Whenever you make a melee attack, make a DE check. If you fail, you fall in and take 1D3 H-DMG. If you pass, make a ST check as well. If you pass, you push the monster in and they are out of the battle.
4	**Brambles**	B	The tangled brambles make it difficult to move. +1 on DE checks.
5	**Thorns**	T	Thorns coat the ground. Make a DE check before each round of combat or take 1D2 H-DMG.
6	**Sunlight**	S	Sun still manages to shine through the trees. If the Sunset Points are 5 or lower, earn 1D6 Willpower back up to your max.

Woods Monsters

#	Monster	Max	H-DMG	W-DMG	LF
1	No Monster	–	–	–	–
2	No Monster	–	–	–	–
3	Field Rat	6	1	1	1
4	Grass Snake	6	1	1D2	2
5	Grey Fox	5	1D2	1D2	5
6	White Wolf	4	1D3+1	1D3	7
7	Crawling Hand	6	1D3	1D6	3
8	Possessed Farmer	2	1D3+1	1	10
9	Giant White Wolf	1	1D6	1D6+1	15

This dungeon doesn't have a boss. Instead, the
goal is to find your way out of the woods
without getting killed. Remember to add your
Sunset modifier to your monster roll.

Section 6.0

Ivrad

Finally stumbling out of the woods, pack in hand, you are relieved to see the stone buildings of a town in the distance. Darkness is quickly enveloping the land and you rush across a small wooden bridge into town. A single wooden sign hangs from a pole announcing the village of Ivrad. This is where the driver was supposed to drop you off. You make a mental note to make a complaint against the driver when you get back to London.

Walking down the single dirt street, you notice there aren't many buildings in this place. A few huts and farmhouses dot the landscape. The only public location is a multi-story stone Inn off to one side of the road. It looks like it was once an outpost or watchtower of sorts back in the medieval period. Now it has been converted into a place for travelers, though you doubt many come this way.

In the distance, the cathedral dwarfs the rest of the village in its shadow. Moonlight creates an eerie glow about the building.

You wonder for a moment if you should head straight to the cathedral and report to Father Tavers who requested the Order's presence. However, you decide maybe it is getting too late. After all, hunting evil after dark isn't always a good idea.

Gripping the handle of your leather travel bag, you instead turn toward the stone building of the Inn. After stumbling and crawling through the woods, you are looking forward to a hot meal, maybe some ale or beer, and the warmth of a soft straw bed.

Section 6.1

The Crow's Inn

A single gas lantern burns on the outside of the building as you approach, illuminating the worn wooden sign. The Crow's Inn.

Stepping through the wooden front door, you are taken aback to see it is mostly dark inside. Except for a single candle that is almost burnt out, the place hides itself in the shadows. There doesn't seem to be anyone up and about. Now that you think of it, it didn't seem like anyone was out and about when you entered the village either. It is almost like the place is deserted.

"Hello? Customer here," you call out. There is no answer.

You step up to the desk to see if there is a bell of some sort, but the flame on the little candle snuffs out. "Damn," you mutter, trying to feel around in the nearly pitch darkness for another candle. You manage to find one, but it is strangely shaped, lumpy, as if crafted by an untrained hand. Deciding it doesn't matter, you retrieve a book of matches from your own pocket.

Striking one, you touch it to the wick of the candle and gasp, nearly stumbling back. The candle is awful in appearance. It has a carving of some sort of monster or gargoyle made into the wax. What sort of candle is this?

Looking over to where you grabbed it, you see a wooden display pedestal that is labeled: "The Ancient Candle of the Dead. DO NOT LIGHT."

"You fool! You damn fool!" Someone whispers angrily.

You hold up the candle to see an old woman

with a shawl over her head staring at you from the staircase behind the desk.

"You stupid fool," she says in a thick German accent. "Now they will awaken. After all these years, they will awaken and seek their master."

You may now ask the woman questions:

- **Who Are You?** The woman doesn't seem to have time to answer questions and waves you off. "You must stop them. It is up to you now."
- **May I Have a Room for the Night?** "No, you may not, you fool," she says. "Sleep in the barn for all I care."
- **What is This Candle?** "It is the Candle of the Dead, you fool. Now they will awaken and seek out their master. You must stop them before they can."
- **Who Will Awaken?** "It awakens the Knights of Blood. The long dead men who serve Lord VanDrac. You must go to the cathedral now. They will be coming out of their Crypts. Stop them. You must stop them." With that, she rushes off up the

stairs and you hear a door slam.

Section 7.0

The Holy Father Cathedral

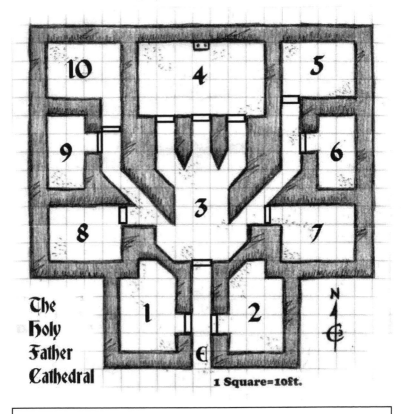

The Holy Father Cathedral

1 Square=10ft.

Knowing you won't be getting a room for the night, you take the candle with you and head toward the Cathedral. If the woman speaks the truth, you are in for a long night. You say a little prayer as you approach the building with its high bell tower. However, you are curious to hear this is all somehow

connected to Lord VanDrac, a name you heard
on your last investigation at the Mother's
Light Abbey where supposedly the Lord's
skull had been kept. Now, it seems, this
candle and whatever it awakens is also
connected to this long dead lord. You'll
need your strength, so you quickly munch on
some food from your satchel you forgot you
had and regain 2D6 Health and Will.

The Holy Father Cathedral is a preconstructed
dungeon map. Each room has a number and a
corresponding entry here in the book. You
start at the entryway labeled **E.** During
gameplay, you will skip the steps for
generating rooms, # of doors, and room type.
Instead, enter the room and read the text box
for the room's entry. Then immediately roll
for monsters. Once all monsters in a room are
defeated, you may then proceed to read the
room's other text. Additionally, whenever you
move through a doorway that is marked on the
map, make a door roll as usual. This is for all
doors except for the ones in rooms **10, 5, 8,**
and **7** which are all automatically "Locked."
Follow the normal procedure for unlocking
doors with a WI check.

Special Rule: Candle of the Dead: You carry
the candle of the dead with you. You may not

set it down and may therefore not wield two melee weapons. It feeds off of your fear. After each bravery check in combat, if you failed that check, the candle burns down a little farther. Keep track of how much it burns. Then, after each battle, roll 2D6. Treat one dice as 10s and one as 1s. (For example: a roll of 6 [60 on the 10s dice] and 3 [3 on the 1s dice] would equal 63). If this die roll is less than the amount of "Candle Burns Down" points, the candle goes out. You are plunged into darkness and the candle's evil magic is complete. All monsters in the cathedral have their Life Force doubled. Their H–DMG and W–DMG deal +1 damage. Additionally, in the darkness all your attacks are done at +1. Your bravery rolls are also made at +1.

Cathedral Doorways		
(6)	Unlocked	Move through freely.
(4–5)	Stuck	Must make a ST check to get through. Lose 1 WILL to reroll and try again.
(1–3)	Locked	Must make a WI check to get through. Lose 1 WILL to reroll and try again.

Cathedral Monsters					
#	Monster	Max	H-DMG	W-DMG	LF
1	Large Rat	5	1D2	1D3	4
2	Vampire Bat	4	1D3	1D3+1	3
3	Guard Dog	3	1D6	1D3	7
4	Satanic Choir Boy	3	1D3+1	1D3+1	7
5	Wicked Priest	1	1D3+1	1D6	8
6	High Cultist	1	1D6	1D6	9

The boss of this dungeon isn't listed here.
Instead, the boss will be listed with the room
description as you enter it.

Room 1: Bishop's Office

This cramped room's centerpiece is a large oak desk. All the walls of the room are covered with floor to ceiling bookshelves filled with books on spiritual matters.

Perusing the shelves, you notice some odd titles.

Make a WITS check now.
- **If you pass:** Read the text box below.
- **If you fail:** Skip it.

While at first glance, most of these books would seem like something normal for a man of the cloth, a closer look reveals books on the topics of necromancy, the undead, blood sacrifices, possession, and more. Is the bishop of this cathedral simply researching the enemy to be prepared for battles with hell, or does he have a darker interest in these topics? You are beginning to wish you'd been able to find Father Tavers before starting into this mess. After all, he'd been the one who sent for you. Did he suspect his own archbishop of fowl play? Where could Father Tavers be now? You pray he isn't dead at the hands of evil.

Room 2: Cathedra

This room is elegant but doesn't have much in it--rich red carpets with gold tapestries hang on the walls. Against the far wall is a large bishop's throne, also known as a Cathedra. In medieval times, the Cathedra might have been out in the chapel. Nowadays, however, it acts like a piece of history here in this room.

Make a WI roll now.

- **If you pass:** Read the text in the box below.
- **If you fail:** Skip it.

Your medieval history comes back to you and you remember that sometimes there were hidden compartments inside of a Cathedra. You decide to go look and sure enough, you are able to pop open a back panel on the Cathedra. In it is a scroll. It speaks of 4 great knights of renown. Each wore a sigil of one of the 4 elements. Each dedicated themselves to their Lord and master. . . Lord VanDrac. It was said they'd ride into the afterlife with him and protect him even in death. This could mean being willing to die themselves when he died . . . or protecting his grave well after death.

Room 3: The Foyer

This room is quiet and has an air of sanctuary about it. Hallways branch off in multiple directions, indicating that this is the center of the building. Benchs sit against walls, available for parishioners waiting for church services to begin. Right now, however, the room is deathly silent.

You may stop at any point in this room to heal 1D6 health and 1D6 willpower, but at the penalty of the candle burning down 1 point.

Room 4: The Chapel

Surprisingly, you'd expect this room to feel comforting and safe, much like the foyer. However, there is a strange foreboding that hangs in the air between the pews. Tall skinny stained glass windows line the far side of the room and they depict gruesome acts of violence from the bible.

In the back of the room on the raised stand behind the altar is a ladder. It appears to go up into the bell tower. However, the trap door at the very top of the ladder is locked. It has 4 keyholes on it. One Iron. One Silver. One Copper. One Gold. If you have the matching keys, you may enter the bell tower (7.1).

Room 5: Northeast Crypt

The Door to this room is locked and requires a Will check.

You cough as you step into this room. The scent of dust, decay, and death invades your nose. The room is mostly stone with a large sarcophagus in the center. A symbol of a drop of water is carved into it. As you approach, the heavy lid scrapes loudly. Sitting up in the coffin in a long dead knight with blue adornments. While he is mostly skeleton and rotting armaments, his eyes glow with blue flame and his skull is fanged like a vampire. You must fight the blue knight now.

Monster	Max	H-DMG	W-DMG	LF
Blue Knight	1	1D6	1D6	15

	Bloodletting	Power
Blue Knight Vampiric Powers	1	3

Once the Blue Knight is dead, you find the Gold Key.

Room 6: Confessional

This room contains a large double doored cabinet you recognize as a confessional--a place where sinners come to confess to their priest and to God. However, so far, based on your impressions of this place, you wonder how much Godliness is left.

If you wish to confess your sins, make a CH roll now, but the candle reduces by 1.

- **PASS:** Blessings upon you child. You heal 2D6 Health and Willpower each and gain 1 Faith.
- **FAIL:** There is no God here. Lose 1D3 Faith and the candles reduces an additional 1.

Room 7: Southeast Crypt

The Door to this room is locked and requires a Will check.

This room smells of old rot. The room is mostly stone with a large sarcophagus in the center. A symbol of a tornado is carved into it. As you approach, the heavy lid scrapes loudly. Sitting up in the coffin in a long dead knight with white adornments. While he is mostly skeleton and rotting armaments, his eyes glow with white flame and his skull is fanged like a vampire. You must fight the white knight now.

Monster	Max	H-DMG	W-DMG	LF
White Knight	1	1D6	1D6	10

White Knight Vampiric Power	Bloodletting	Power
	1	4

Once the White Knight is dead, you find the Silver Key.

Room 8: Southwest Crypt

Ancient cobwebs hang all through this room.
The room is mostly stone with a large
sarcophagus in the center. A symbol of a tree
is carved into it. As you approach, the heavy
lid scrapes loudly. Sitting up in the coffin
in a long dead knight with green
adornments. While he is mostly skeleton and
rotting armaments, his eyes glow with green
flame and his skull is fanged like a
vampire. You must fight the green knight
now.

Monster	Max	H-DMG	W-DMG	LF
Green Knight	1	1D6	1D6	15

Green Knight Vampiric Power	Bloodletting	Power
	2	2

Once the Green Knight is dead, you find the
Iron Key.

Room 9: Sacramental Preparation Room

This room contains shelves, a wash basin, wine, and food stores for use in the preparation of communion and sacrament.

After completing this room, instead of a treasure roll, you earn 1 bread crust and 1 wine.

Room 10: Northwest Crypt

This room smells the oldest of all the rooms you've been in so far. The room is mostly stone with a large sarcophagus in the center. A symbol of a flame is carved into it. As you approach, the heavy lid scrapes loudly. Sitting up in the coffin in a long dead knight with red adornments. While he is mostly skeleton and rotting armaments, his eyes glow with red flame and his skull is fanged like a vampire. You must fight the red knight now.

Monster	Max	H-DMG	W-DMG	LF
Red Knight	1	1D6	1D6	15

Red Knight Vampiric Power	Bloodletting	Power
	2	3

Once the Red Knight is dead, you find the Copper Key.

Section 7.1

The Bell Tower

Unlocking the upper trap door into the bell tower, you climb to the highest point of the cathedral. Emerging onto the platform, you are amazed about the size of the bell. Five or six fully grown men could easily fit inside of the bell's mouth. The bell hangs over a large square opening to the chapel floor way down below. It would be quite a nasty fall.

Suddenly, you hear a sniveling voice. "Impossible. You can't have gotten here."

Moving around the bell, you see a tiny many with a large knobbing hump for a back. The bones of his head seem oddly shaped and uneven. One eye protrudes grotesquely.

You quickly notice two things about him. One, he wears the robes of a priest. Second, in his hands he clutches a skull . . . a skull with vampire fangs.

"It's impossible," the man repeats. "The knights should have killed you."

You quickly deduce that this is Father Taver's, the man who called The Order to report strange paranormal goings on at the cathedral.

"Oh, well. It doesn't matter. I'll kill you myself," he hisses. Removing his outer robe, he reveals a red raven crest. He draws a huge sword with a red hilt. His eyes flare red and you see fangs pop out. He's a vampire.

You must now fight Father Tavers.

While fighting in the Bell Tower, each time you succeed at a melee attack, roll 2D6. On a roll of 2, you manage to push Father Tavers over the edge and down to the room below. This immediately ends the fight.

Additionally, when you fail at a melee attack and after you take damage, make a DE check to not get pushed over the edge. If you fail, make a second DE check to grab onto the bell and swing back up into the room. If you fail the second DE check, you fall down into the chapel below and take 2D6 H-DMG. If you are still alive, make your way back up to the tower to continue the fight.

Monster	Max	H-DMG	W-DMG	LF
Father Tavers	1	2D6	2D6	15

	Bloodletting	Power
Father Tavers Vampiric Power	3	3

Section 8.0

Ending the Adventure

Striking one final blow against Father Tavers, the hunchback lets out a bellowing scream and falls down from the tower. You rush to the ladder and climb down into the chapel below. However, when you reach the bottom there is no sign of Father Tavers OR the vampire skull he was carrying.

A flutter of wings echoes in the air and you can only guess he turned into a bat that flew away. You have a feeling this isn't the last you'll see of him . . . or the last you'll hear of this supposed Lord VanDrac. Who is he and why does he seem to have so many servants who serve him even in death?

Glancing down at the spent Candle of the Dead, you see that encased within the wax was a bone . . . a rib. You have a sick feeling that this bone, too, might belong to Lord VanDrac. You guess that perhaps Father Tavers called you here for fear that you and the Order were getting too close to figuring out what is happening with Lord VanDrac. He clearly hoped to kill you.

However, you now have one more clue to take back with you to the Order's labs for investigation and testing. You are betting this is indeed a bone of a vampire.

Stepping out of the cathedral, the morning light breaks across the small town. The old lady of the inn comes out. "Praise the Lord," she cries, rushing forward and hugging you. Other town people emerge, grateful to you for ridding their village of the evil that had oppressed them. It all started when Father Tavers started taking an interest in The Candle of the Dead. Seems the lore is only someone of pure faith can light the candle. Maybe that was why he sent for you?

The villagers gather up a collection of money to thank you for your service and you receive 2D6x5 pounds.

Hammer✠Cross

Character Record Sheet

Name: **Order:**   **Class:**

STATS

St   De   Wi   Ch

Proficiency:

WEAPONS

Ranged: **Melee:**

ARMOR   ITEMS

WILL   HEALTH   FAITH   £

Made in the USA
Monee, IL
12 August 2021

75546925R00028